Praise for *These Spaceships Weren't Built for Us*

I0795194

"This that late night backseat soundscape while the homie maintains the wheel. *These Spaceships Weren't Built for Us* is that wondrous ride with a last look in the rearview. Adjust the mirror. What do you see? "I don't mean to be so American, / but I am," Alan Chazaro writes as he traverses and meditates on the various borders of our lives. Follow the music. Lean into the bass. What do you feel? "There is a boneyard of buildings / inside my chest—" he proclaims. This is that voyage through all we've been framed by—be it bicycle spokes, eucalyptus roots, or collapse—the good, the bad, and the neon. I'm down for these poems, and down for Chazaro when he says, "What / is exploration without desperation?" Come thru, kick it. We're all here already."

—Michael Torres, author of *An Incomplete List of Names*

"Alan Chazaro is the bard of the Bay, the bard of the barrio. Like my late grandfather, Chazaro keeps time recalling cars and songs from the past. They mark time like tree rings. They unlock portals of memory like the vinyl ridges on a record. His poems create temporal shifts and catalog neighborhood histories from Oakland to Jackson Heights. The poems are laced with references just for the homies. They're shoutouts. With *These Spaceships Weren't Built for Us*, Chazaro transforms the ranfla, the hooptie, and the G-ride into a spaceship, | a time machine. He points our gaze to the sky and we long to take flight while simultaneously holding onto our roots and what keeps our feet on the ground."

—Joseph Rios, Fresno Poet Laureate and author of *Shadowboxing: Poems & Impersonations*

"A poet, teacher, and journalist, Alan's writings reek of a well-traveled critical thinker who hasn't forgotten how to imagine a brighter future. In *These Spaceships Weren't Built for Us*, the Bay Area-bred wordsmith shows us where he's from, where he wants to go, and places no human has ever been. The running theme of space travel takes to a new perspective as it's painted by the words of a Mexican American man who loves lyrical hip-hop, culturally rich cuisine, and his family. The subject matter of Alan's writing—identity and immigration, reckoning with the past and trying to make a better tomorrow—speaks to the issues of today. And in this book, Alan makes it clear: those themes will continue to resonate as long as this spaceship we're flying through the cosmos, continues to operate this way."

—Pendarvis Harshaw, journalist and author of *OG Told Me*

"Alan Chazaro's latest collection *These Spaceships Weren't Built for Us* cannot be more timely and necessary as it generates important discussions with lines like 'I wonder how many borders are crossed without us ever knowing' and 'resistance is not letting anyone inside because resistance is a burning.' *These Spaceships Weren't Built for Us* honors the language of our abuelas remixed with the sounds from the Bay Area as we explore galaxies that can only be designed by Chazaro."

–Luivette Resto, *Living on Islands Not Found on Maps*

These Spaceships Weren't Built For Us

POEMS

Alan Chazaro

TIA CHUCHA PRESS
Los Angeles

ISBN 978-1-882688-65-4

Book Design: Jane Brunette
Cover Art: Alfonso Juarez

PUBLISHED BY:
Tía Chucha Press
A Project of Tia Chucha's Centro Cultural, Inc.
PO Box 328
San Fernando CA 91341

www.tiachucha.org/tia-chuchas-press

These Spaceships Weren't Built for Us *by Alan Chazaro is part of the Letras Latinas Publishing Collaborative. Established in 2026, the Collaborative formalized the ties between Letras Latinas and the constellation of community-minded presses who publish works by Latinx writers with the assistance of a Letras Latinas subvention. Letras Latinas is the literary initiative at the University of Notre Dame's Institute for Latino Studies.*

HERE

THERE

contents

GONE

for future readers
in a future world

for Maceo

here

Spacesuit, or Learning How to Float through Public Space

I'm somewhere between high and low
altitudes right now—where the snow begins

to bear-hug a rising surface and the outside looks
like a gentle suffocation. I don't

mean to suggest there is violence
happening. I mean to say these branches

can become instruments for the body.
That rocks and cold air can carry more

than our breath. I'm where Ashland, Oregon, borders
California's limits, though there isn't

much change across state lines. I wonder
how many borders are crossed without us

ever knowing. I wonder if these signs are signaling
more than our current elevation. A Tribe

Called Quest vibrates from the back
of my skulled memory. David explains the origins

of *vaporwave* while my phone slow-
dies. I keep responding to brightly illuminated

text messages, but there are hundreds
of miles left to go. I'm in the backseat

of a Toyota Corolla caught in forward motion.
I'm somewhere between high and low, and

I've lost count of the bridges
we've slipped beneath.

Fanny points to the wingspan of a hawk, points
at a car we passed earlier. I didn't notice but notice

how many buildings are ghosted between Portland
and San Francisco, machinery and big-wheeled

work trucks expanding across this slippery spectrum.
Imagine the darkest bodies in our solar system

without any light to interrupt them.
What's the longest you've ever held

your breath? Are you
still holding? A part of the Sierra forest is gone, chunked

into nearby log stacks along the road. A playlist
of Bay Area rap never ends,

like rainfall but I don't feel
trapped by this. I feel the pouring,

the downward rumble. This isn't necessarily bad—
falling. Isn't that how the ancients once wrote about the beginning

of our attraction? I was told that when we're born
we're already in a fallen position, so we must learn

how to undo this by walking. I was told we are given
one body to fall into, so we must learn quickly.

On the Way to Ojai

I don't know how to say what needs saying, so I'll say
this instead. It's about orange orchards and vineyards
huddled beneath the Santa Ynez mountains. About migrant
laborers, their bodily distance
from the main road. It's about the nearby desert's
blush, my privilege
in watching men and women bend over bundles
of lettuce while I drive through Trump territory—where Blue Lives Matter
flags and Confederate symbology sprout
from dirt. I don't mean to be so American,
but I am. I'm on my way to Ojai, gliding
along central California's axis. The sprinklers are squirting
and the workers are oceans in the open fields. Air conditioning
keeps me cool as Too $hort blaps from my Ford's
metaphorical grill. I admit: it's the first time
I've driven these parts. At the gas station, a white man
tells me I don't need to wear my mask around here. He looks
me directly in the eyes.

Post-Apocalyptic Pastoral at Lake Merritt in Oakland

Pretending to be a ghost here is nothing

new—I am wandering without a body—

there is a boneyard of buildings

inside my chest—I don't know

what *exogenous* means,

but it somehow calls my name—

across broken waters,

shadow-clouds gather—where sky-

scrapers used to stretch toward an open

ceiling, there is now absence—like missing

teeth—how can I unbraid toxicity

from my scalp?—what if memory

is more than a tangle of nerves

wiring my ribs?—the opposite of this

is skinning a pomegranate

with your survival

instincts—it's the crush of organic

seeds in clenched jaws—

it's the chewing—the red juices.

My Mexican Abuela Taught Me How to Land on the Moon

When I first kissed
my abuela's language, it felt like I was floating on a third

moon. Some people say we've never even landed

on the first moon. Some people think the world isn't really

globed. I don't believe in flatness and rarely consider gravity

unless I'm falling.   Maybe I should.   Have you ever been so unsatisfied

with the present that you present yourself with a solution that doesn't
make sense?

A city in China proposed to build a replica

of the moon
and hang it

like a photograph

framed in the night sky. They said it would hold

the city's light in times of darkness

to conserve energy.   What if conserving energy

was actually a bad thing? What if we never cleansed

our mouths of whatever needed saying? I guess I'm not sure

if there's ever a perfect

moment. If there's more to this

than strangled breaths   and emptiness, if we simply imagine

whatever we want for ourselves—impossible forms

of comfort. When my abuelita passed

I didn't cry. She gave me

her impossible comfort from two feet away. She gave me many moons

in my upturned palms. When I need her,

I return to their many surfaces. They keep me grounded

with impossibilities.

What the Alien Tried Saying in a Language He Does Not Speak

Lately, I am walking backward
into myself. Lately, I am unspoken.

Nepantla spoken
backward is liberation.

The U.S. territories
around my tongue are bordered.

Resistance is not letting anyone
inside because resistance is a burning.

My abuela's lengua
is the result of someone else's violence.

This is an alternate way
of saying *forced*
entry, another sound
for *memoria*.

I dream in inverted silhouettes
of ¿ and dip into galaxies
above *ñ*.

My alphabet is a scarring
of air, the breaking of
unsplit lips.

I asked a machista what he believed
about bullet-pointed
honesty. He answered with
bullets.

I should've asked
if he's ever learned
how to unswallow
his own songs.

Give me more and I'll untether myself
from this; give me less and I'll speak
in a body unbroken by punctuations.

An Introduction to American Pathology (Remix)

I'm lost and wandering in a forest of blue gum
eucalyptus trees and fog horns in San Francisco

while listening to Baby Keem's *The Sound*
of Bad Habit. I'm thinking about which X-Men

I'd be if I could choose between
each character (none are Latino):

Cyclops, Wolverine, Magneto, Nightcrawler,
Professor X. I haven't imagined

beyond that. Maybe I'll start a band and name it
ULTRA DARK GALACTIC WOLF.

Isn't naming something a type of self-love? I don't understand
how the world slow-reveals itself to us, how

the damaged moon returns every week-
night, sickled. Daily, I hoard fragments

of my hours like an unsolved litany: Hisoka
from *Hunter x Hunter*; Kyle's U.S. Army veteran

tattoos; in-flight turbulence from Spokane
to the Oakland airport; small creases in the leather

fabric of my Jordan 1s; my wife's cousin who works
as a prison guard in North Dakota to pay

for his college tuition. I look to my left and see crimson. I look
to my right and see vanilla. Funny part is

I'm not a good fighter, but I often find myself
in good fights. Funny part is we're all

in this fight now. It's not that complicated:
I no longer know what's killing me or what

part of me is turning
neon. I no longer trust the shadows in our hills.

A Portrait of Kevin Durant Leaving the Brooklyn Nets

I'm wearing an orange knit beanie, a camouflage
North Face fleece and a pair of Nike Uptempo sneakers
I bought in Mexico from a group of men
who smelled like frequently exchanged pesos
inside a vacant room. Back
in California, I'm walking on 23rd Avenue, past
the houseless dude who looks at me and flicks
his thumb in the shape of a lighter. I don't have
gasoline, don't carry a dollar, but tell him I'll bless
him on my way out. I get cash inside the liquor store
to put inside his palms, but when I return, he's ghosted. Everything
moves fast here. Bicycle spokes,
police cruisers, the man who parks his Impala
in front of grandma's house but never rolls down
his tinted windows. Sometimes I give him a head nod and his hair
shines back. He has two English Mastiffs that he keeps
off-leash. It's cold and warm at the same time. The San Pablo Bay cuts
along the edges of our neighborhood, pushing the salt and smoke and oil
from the nearby Chevron refinery into our tracheas. It's autumn
during a pandemic. My phone vibrates with empty messages.
My head is overheated and everything is a jigsaw.
I scroll through Twitter and see Kevin Durant
in a retro Nets jersey, half-smiling.

It’s 9:44PM and I’m Listening to “7AM” by Playboi Carti

because I’m bored and everything is static. Earlier, I rambled around IKEA

in Emeryville, wearing a mask. I picked up plushie dinosaurs and rearranged

the leather chairs and dish racks while pretending they could fit

somewhere inside my mind. I went home empty-handed then fixed

the broken taillights on my Volkswagen. I hit up Home Depot

and picked up a door to install in our bedroom. I spent half an hour

watching a YouTube video called “How To Cut Perfect Door Hinges.”
I learned

about the recesses on the flat of a door jamb, about mortises

and palm routers. By nightfall, Bernardo was outside mowing the lawn.

Grandma says, *His yard work is beautiful.* He used to live

in the back shed, slept with our tools. He lived somewhere

else after that and we’d sometimes see him around. He rode his bicycle

on our street while my AirPods were in. He is no longer with us.

Pocho Boy Escapes the Internet to Explore Machu Picchu

On the fifth day, I managed to crawl while tossing clouds
from cliff sides because ruins aren't really ruined
until they tilt into the earth. I've wandered
miles to carry this, chased falling
stars as if they wouldn't crash atop my dome
for this. When I awoke, coca leaves and dirt were mixed
in my lungs. The mist deletes every path
behind me, and in front there is a patch of untamed
bamboo growing. I've seen how grass
can be used to build bridges by using only fingers
and knees—if you twist anything tight enough
it might hold you up, too. If you look deeper
into the water you might see the cosmos
pooling in your reflection, a dialect forming
from the sweet mud around you. This morning
I tasted altitude on my tongue. I felt the highest forest
take root in me. I rock-stepped across an ancient road
not meant for our feet. I lost
my torso at the summit and held my breathing
close to the rib cage. Never forget
about the river and never forget about
the distance. Trust that this elevation is meant for us.

Late Night as Pocho Boy

While everyone slept, I'd watch the skulls
of my idols scrape against a muted sky. I'm talking

NBA Jam—Latrell Sprewell and Chris Webber
as digital duo. I'm speaking post-Christmas

boyhood tongue and video game cartridges
undusted. Sophomore year: I started

pinning photos of muscle cars next to posters
of Tyra Banks in bikinis. Relaxation

suddenly became a synonym for self-touching. How
the first time a friend of a friend came over she laid

wordlessly across my bed. How the language
of knowing escaped me.

How I wasn't sure where to go.
Back when I would draw circles

in the margins of random notebooks in the back
of class. Back when I failed

and was failed. Because I've never been fast
at learning. Because I was only good at observing

Shawn Kemp climb impossible pyramids
of air. Because in those years, everything was

and wasn't a game. I scored and I didn't.
I'm still learning how to miss.

California Roll

On weekends, I enjoy listening to slowed-down versions of myself.

On repeat, anything sounds good. Birds flock nearby

the shore. We are falling short of greatness,

whatever that means. I started shaving the sides of my head

during quarantine. Someone asked if I was a soccer player. I'm not.

My family gathers in small settings: a backyard, Coronas,

the 49ers, masks never on. You can't slow this drip. I ride

the wave hoping not to drown. Months ago, my cousin invited me

to L.A. I stayed inside his apartment. He rolled Kush every morning

with his brown fingers. The beach was waiting for us.

It's still there.

A Loose Dissertation on Movement with Souls of Mischief as Soundtrack

I'm carrying distant shores

on my fingertips though I don't

know what mileage I've left

behind me. I've inherited

this loss of sunlight, the sleepless

wonders of a foreigner.

I'm in a labyrinth of cempasúchil,

and everything is breathing.

I promise you: this lyric

is covered in the honey

of a Mexican serape

in winter. It's the birth

of a candlelight's truth.

Hygge means you don't know

what's beneath the open-aired

courtyard until you've come up

for more air. I won't

call for breath

until I've lived

beyond myself. Pour me

a double round

of wet afternoons and basketball

courts near subway stations.

Watch the snow

dribble into streaks

across your double-laced hoodie.

This is where I want to fold

into nothing I can pronounce.

This is how I want to chill

from 93 'til Infinity. This is

why I take free throws as if it matters.

Red Cloud Litany

In Richmond, a red cross is burning
over a Methodist Church. This isn't a metaphor.

If you reach the land's end, you can see it all:
the Bay Bridge; Mount Tamalpais; fishermen

overlooking anchored yachts; warehouses and
shipyards. What else does this place hold?

Today is the shade of erasure. Maybe apocalypse,
in a literal sense. I feel the grim reaper ready

to reap without a whisper. I'm horrified but grab
my camera and hop over a chain link fence.

I aim my shutter and click. I don't want to forget
what it felt like when we were buried.

there

"Space can be interesting without being an astronaut"

is something I once overheard a mother telling

her little boy at the Space Center in Houston / He didn't

respond, just kept playing with the toy in his small

clutches / I came here not knowing what I wanted

but found it / Example: *methods for reaching*

extreme altitudes / Example: Goddard's

Rocket, built in the 13th century, using gunpowder

as fuel / I wonder what sound is made when our ambition

punctures the stratosphere / I listen to the darkest

corners but only hear insecurities / The first American to command

orbit was Alan B. Shepard / 1961 / What did Earth tell him

when he looked down upon it? / What finally disrupted

his gaze? / When discussing safety,

an astronaut said, *If we waited until it was*

safe we would never do it / I admit I'm afraid to risk

most leaps of discovery / When I learned about two

NASA missions that resulted in the loss

of human life, I somehow wasn't saddened / There are only so many
spaces left to search / The macro and the micro / What
is exploration without desperation? /
How can you worship triumph
without praising the technology
of defeat? / I want to be above
this ground while staying grounded / Who doesn't? / I want
the gravity of many worlds combined
with mine / Don't you? / I'm holding this
under a thick Southern rainfall / Apparently
the world is eating its own oceans / Meanwhile we're eating
each other's hunger / *Lift off* is a phrase that implies altering
the physics of whatever you've known about any surface / On
the subject of the Hubble Space Telescope, I learned *the images*
it sends back to Earth allow humanity to peer deeper
into the cosmos / I want to peer deeper into
our circuitries / At some point, a final astronaut will be launched
into space / A singularity / A song
of hope or abandonment? / We all carry space boots with us,

we just don't know it yet / If we ever travel far enough

beyond the known frontier, [insert blank] / Have you ever noticed

how space is portrayed in movies as endlessly frigid? /

As spectacularly reachable?

16 Reasons Why a DACA Dreamer Will Be the First Person to Build a Do-It-Yourself Spaceship from Simple Materials

1: Because Dreamers already know how to work under atmospheric pressure.

2: Because according to the dictionary, *If you describe someone as a dreamer, you mean that they spend a lot of time thinking about and planning for things that they would like to happen but which are improbable or impractical*, and what's less practical than being 52,000 altitudes out of reach?

3: Because *flying* means learning how to lift yourself off the angles of a planet with nothing to keep you afoot.

4: Because when Adrian was deported, he told me he would go far away; and I'm not sure he meant Mexico City; and I'm not sure he wanted to leave; and I'm not sure that after living for decades in California he wasn't more American than my blue Levi's, more American than Max's white Mustang convertible, more American than listening to the red noise of Jimmy Hendrix's National Anthem in Guillermo's bedroom after school; I've never been sure.

5: Because how else can you transcend these burning grids?

6: Because Dreamers have also been called *aliens* since birth. And, well, aliens know how to build spaceships, right?

7: Because our government states, *Under this version of the DREAM Act, immigrants could qualify in part, by meeting the following requirements: Be[ing] between the ages of 12 and 35 at the time the Law is enacted [and] arriv[ing] in the United States before the age of 16*, as if asking a child to keep dreaming into adulthood isn't some form of psychological colonization, as if Dreamers won't eventually wake up.

8: Because when civilizations are magicked from mud, futures can happen while stargazing from a naked rooftop.

9: Because fuck Donald Trump—3.6 million times, one for each Dreamer.

10: Because whenever Kanye West rapped on his first album, *The College Dropout*, we'd parrot along in the backseat of my brother's 1996 Jetta on Highway 101, our windows down, the wind passing by, a squad of Mexican-blooded boys learning how to embrace the Bay Area's cold warmth as our own: *I've been / workin' this grave shift / and I ain't made shit / I wish I could / buy me a spaceship and fly—*

11: Because everyone I know who's a Dreamer has only ever given and given and given and given and given and given and still.

12: Because I remember smoking late nights at Sergio's house and seeing his father, uncles, brothers, cousins all rise for work like solar bodies circling the vacant air while the rest of us were entering sleep, when the city was a thick oil spill of te deepest shades of dark, and even deeper than that.

13: Because in the unseenness of space, no one can question your legality.

14: Because there is already a loss of air and gravity in los Estados Jodidos.

15: Because don't Dreamers know what it means to have an expiration on selfhood more than any of us? *On September 5, 2017, President Trump ordered an end to the Deferred Action on Childhood Arrivals (DACA) program. This program shields young undocumented immigrants—who often arrived at a very young age in circumstances beyond their control—from deportation.*

16: Because who else has already traveled between worlds and survived to tell its secrets.

Someone's Astronaut Tio Is Selling a Constellation of Paletas on a Faraway Tropical Planet

because even the fringe planets need the music of cart-pushing paleteros—their voices lifting from wildly-decorated spaceships. And I don't mean to make this about some pocho sci-fi shit. But I will. I'll slide the freshest galactic currency into the gloved palms of someone else's astronaut tío. Because right now I'm inside the paleta multiverse: where paleteros are living their best lives; where they never get assaulted because that would be a communal felony; where they collect unlimited clout and retirement funds for their hustle on a faraway tropical planet. And I say tropical because it's hot there and everyone will need the religion of something cold on a stick to enjoy. And these paleteros will be the most luminous gods we've known. We will praise their frozen galaxies, memorializing their routes like biblical scriptures graffitied onto asteroid belts from here to the luna and back. And nothing will ever melt here. How could it?

What This First-Generation Mexican/American Thinks About When I Think About Space Travel

It's all there: while staring up at star patterns from a backyard at a homie's house party in Oakland with old school Outkast booming in the background and laughing the fullest laugh that my elder millennial bones can hold as Jerome and Andrew are nearby talking about the depths of the Pacific Ocean and a white guy walks up to tell me how strange the shade of the moon looks and mentions how we should, as a society, start over by inhabiting the moon, and how right there, in that smallest of liminal fractures, from that particular angle and with that uncrossable distance between me and this stranger and the moon, how I look up and agree, that yes, it would be ideal to break ground on some distant surface that is somehow shapelier, somehow more perfectly livable and ready for us to unpack our furniture upon while knowing in the furthest cabinet of my insides that when we actually arrive, we'll inhale suffocation all over again.

What Scientists Know About Black Holes

A Quick Death

And I quote: *gravity will drag you*
toward the singularity at the speed of light
and ultimately spaghettify you.

You Need to Travel at Lightspeed to Escape an Event Horizon

Prior to that, what part of you
would celebrate? What part of you
wouldn't?

Astronomers Estimate That Our Galaxy Harbors Approximately 100 Million Black Holes

The spiral of your being might pull me
into an unknown. You can take this
literally or you can take it as metaphor.

Like Planets and Stars, There Are Both Big and Small Black Holes. You Will Die Regardless of What Size of Black Hole You Enter.

This conveniently loops me back to bullet point #1: if you fuck
around enough you might just
find out. Lesson being
there is a limit to this body, to this skin,
to this politic. Keep your hands where I can see them
in America.

How to Trap Light

Hold your hands around it. Let go
when you've noticed the salt
of adrenaline leave your fingers.

When You Only See Darkness, Then You'll Know You're Inside a Black Hole

Because the darker the center the deeper
the truth. Reminds me of when Pac said,
The darker the berry the sweeter
the juice. Because all along we've been thinking
Pac's been in Cuba but maybe he got lost
inside the blackest hole in America.

Physics Break Down

Just like the first car I ever bought in Louisiana,
a black Honda with tinted windows and
black rims. Just like the time I was pulled over
by the New Orleans Police Department for making a legal
turn. Just like how the officers made me step
out of my car and exit myself. Just like their hands feeling
everything about me except how I was feeling.
Just like backup arriving with more undercover
threats, more accusations. Just like how I was a high school
teacher driving my car on a potholed street
on a Tuesday afternoon. Just like how they said they'd take me
to fucking jail that day. Just like their hands crawling my skin.
Just like hands crawling your skin. Just like how they couldn't take me
because I wasn't breaking
any laws. Just like how they still tried to break
me. Just like how they wanted to turn me
against myself. Just like how they had to let me go.
Just like how it only happened to me once, but it taught me
everything I needed to know.

You Might Never Come Back

You don't need an astrophysicist to tell you
when you might not come back.
There is no mathematics for loss.
These days, things haven't been adding up. These

days, I've been feeling subtracted and divided.
It feels like we're curled into a sunken space.
But I also remember how light
explodes brightest when dark.

On Being Evicted from Earth

We are first-generation cadets learning how to unspiral &
environmental denial is a form of imprisonment &
silence is a kind of killer too &
bodies in the inner solar system have already been considered for space
colonization &
the European Space Agency sounds fake but it isn't &
who has the best lunar capabilities? &
that sounds like something Elon Musk would ask &
the only thing I remember from watching Bill Nye on TV is the catchy
intro song but nothing about actual science &
I'm not convinced I should be leaving yet I've already left &
when choosing between planets it's easy to feel displaced &
most days, I'm at a loss for words and my belongings &
I move silently beneath it all because who can afford to buy a home right
now &
maybe that's why I've let go &
if you agree with me blink three times &
if not then let's agree to never blink again &
I've never been able to walk a straight path beneath a crooked sky &
nothing is parallel so I've learned to find pleasure in perpendiculars &
I can't remember the last time we argued, but it must've tasted like candy
before a cavity &
it hasn't rained much in California for years &
I'll interpret that as some kind of alarm &
I'm sensitive to the insensitivity of others &
I feel negative space around me, an astronaut in the void &
I told my wife that this soil is in our veins &
I meant it &
still I'd like to leave &
I've tried to throw away the past but don't know how &
we can barely afford our native planet &
we are now in the hands of an algorithm &
whatever happens on earth will remain with the glaciers.

I Don't Go On TikTok But If I Did I'd Post This

I'm in a room full of mirrors I can't see
myself in because they've warped
with centuries of sharded truths.
In Buenos Aires, I'm holding an antique
globe in my hands like I've never known
its circular weight, like borders have never been
drawn or redrawn. Everywhere
is discolored and fading. There is a scent
of fire but no smoke. A soft-spoken
grandmother offers me handmade
handkerchiefs that bloom
like gardens in faraway mouths. She notices
a stain on the fabric and lowers
her price. I buy it to wear
as a bandana except it doesn't
hold tightly, so I wrap
the cloth around my neck
like a European aristocrat. Nearby, across

the teeth of a river, there is an abandoned

coliseum. It holds the dead

art of bullfighting, where matadores once kicked

their own dust to the applause

of skeletal crowds. No one goes inside

anymore. Instead, we take

selfies while smiling

in front of the entrance. Every day, locals

must walk past this history and never

flinch. Every time I meet tourists they ask,

Where are you from? I tell them *California* then

disappear from their orbits. How many times

have you locked eyes with a stranger

and felt known? When you get into a taxi

what do you fantasize about? A forgotten

countryside is moving in my windows,

but I rarely look up. My time is a subtle

carnival of sound and flavor—beef,

liquor, nighttime. I'm chasing after

nothing with Mac Dre circa 2004

inside my earphones. Briana says

it feels like we're walking toward paradise

on a rusty steel bridge. I don't

disagree.

gone

Pocho Boy Builds the Spaceship

for Briana

So, when I finally go into orbit I'd like
to be listening to something like

A$AP Mob's *Cozy Tapes Vol. 2: Too Cozy*:
the sounds of bass and Harlem's

adlibs ultra-blasting
through the stratosphere

(a cinematic sequence in my mind)
engineered with the highest

tech precision while there are
inessential beeping noises in the back-

ground. And when I go from here,
I'd like to pretend

it's something I knew
I'd always do—like the time I left

the West Coast for the Deep South
or when I asked for my first

pack of grape-flavored
Optimos at my neighborhood

corner store. And in that moment
of liminality I'll think,

Damn, this is
the real getaway.

And the world will be aflame.
Why else would we be flying

off elsewhere
if our planet

was still danceable
and not raging

beneath us? And I don't know
much, but I do know this:

when I go, I'd like
to have you

there, too, the trueness
of your shape

nearby, the assurance
of your coldest

jokes. Maybe that's what
I'll need when it all ends.

A Postcard from the Next Dimension

These days are taking me
toward an unclothing, toward
a starburst beneath oiled palm trees
and space drizzle. I'm standing on
the roof of a decayed building, between
the crooked prayers of someone else's
god. I'm looking
down at the city. In the distance, farther
than my eyes can navigate, there's an open
shore. The gravel is thickening
inside me. Wake me up
when it's over, when these ruins and moon
patterns have been mapped. Until then,
I'll tongue coconut water and move
to Bad Bunny with El Espíritu Santo. I'll leave
dirt in my pockets, a labyrinth
I cannot untangle in my throat.

No One Has Ever Told Me To Go Back to My Planet, But If They Did, I'd Roll Up My Space Hoopty's Windows and Listen to "M.E.T.H.O.D. Man"

Simply to feel the air and bounce of my 5th-grade self again. Back when we'd gather around Aldo's boombox like acolytes inside a tucked off

temple in the mighty slums of Shaolin. We did it for the diss tracks and interludes looping uninterrupted in our apartment while Pa worked a full shift. Clockwork,

I'd wake up and listen to Staten Island's superheroes on repeat, studying the Wu's interdimensional arts from East to West Coast during infinity turf wars

in the 90s. Back then, I wandered the *36 Chambers* unknown within me. The secret? We all shared this soundtrack: pochos, Chinitos, Filipinos—

immigrant families near the Bay's shoreline. The smell? Fish oils and faraway spices. Sounds of home, as homely as it can get in this skin. Wherever

I go now, I carry this as a shelter, as I step outside to hold a new sun's diameter between my teeth, reciting RZA's abode psalms

in foreign coordinates while church bells clatter. Believe that I'm ready to conjure a mixtape of revolution and single-parented love with a cassette player stuck

on rewind. It'll be playing everywhere my spaceship drifts while in search of quesadillas and ramen and killer bees.

Alternate Universe Ending #2

In this version I'm riding an all-black
single-gear bike along Lakeshore Ave.

near my apartment and a cadenza
of dusk is guiding the nearby family

of trees into a deep chorus of green
melodies that can only be described

as hymnal, as if
our bodies might be forever

and impossibly loosened
in a wild dance of light.

In this moment I am taken
by a bloom of faces

around me, and I cannot tell if I'm pedaling
forward or being pulled

on a string, or if this connection
stretches far beyond

wherever this sidewalk ends, toward
a dimension I have no business

entering because I am no cosmonaut. I am
unsuited, just a Mexican mother's boy who watches

too much *Star Wars* and wonders: what stardust
will powder me?

Glass Beach Burial While Draped in a Bandana, Because Big Smoke Is In the Air

Northern California is not a daydream—it is
a landfill with signs saying, *Don't turn your back
on the ocean.* For years I've mapped these interstate
lines like tattoos on a body

I never asked for. The saturation
of ink, the hustle
above unbroken bones, the cartilage
housing eucalyptus roots in
a drought. It is the earthquake, and it is

the fire, and there are not enough
beds to sleep in, but still, we burn and dream
of dreams wide enough to hold these redwoods
and coastlines—because everything

here is splitting or has already been
split, and we are laughing
beneath a sunset. There are
layered depths beneath this ground

—which belongs to you? There are many versions
of ourselves along every beachfront—
which do you hold closest? The air
is warm but we wear hoodies. Ice

never haunts our songs but still
we sing. I'm saying this is
and isn't what we want it to be. There are
orchards of unpicked ambition to harvest

inside all of us. We are drawn
to the curvature
of this light. We all
want to rest here.

Millennial World Politics, or Dear Future Self

I am forgetting how to write
about joy because I can't remember how
to unwrap myself from this blanket
of storms we are beginning to call our days.
Look at 2016, 2020, 2024.

This is America, rapped Childish Gambino,
the home of the fully divided and unprovided
for. On Instagram I once heard Spike Jonze
ask his interviewers if they had more hope
in America's progress

or more faith in America's collapse.
Before they could answer, Jonze said he believed
America would find itself again. I don't think
he meant America would find itself again.
I think he meant America would overturn

itself and discover what's underneath, the forgotten
sediments. There have always been
those who praise fire, those with grandfathers
who carried rifles and rope while burning
peace from flesh—but I will not grant them

my bones. I'd rather walk with stains on my clothes,
with saints between my toes, chuckling.
I am relearning what it means to glide
with hidden pleasure in every room I merge into.
There will always be something to hate,

a barely visible scar
sitting above my left knuckle.
I do not yet understand each morning's arrival, rituals

amid ongoing brutalism. What have we become
if not bridges suspending the next generation's doom?

I want to give more than myself. To build
a sanctuary of tamales and agua de jamaica
for you. I was taught beauty
is not yours nor mine to keep. I used to avoid
scuffs on my sneakers. Bilingual

disassociation is my own kind of weird country.
Somehow, a teenage boy wearing a hoodie while walking in
America is a promise America can't always keep.
I make eye contact and say, *What's up?*
to the brimmed hats with shielded eyes. I only want

what we can inhale
with our collective lungs. I want to hold that in me
and in you and you and you.
Maybe it will be granted,
and maybe it won't.

Song of Revival in New York City While My Father is Asleep Beside Me

Last night I chased jungle birds and found my way

through an obtuse lens. Tomorrow

I will unbury my fingers

from previous defeats. A truth: I'm beginning

to feel electric, observing the operatic

announcements of a Hydrangea—what about you?

I'm arrested and unable to rest.

A flooded subway station. My iPhone

with a cracked screen. Confession: I want more

than this collection of Travis Scott's Nike releases

at Flight Club. I want an intimate cartography,

a mapping of irregular terrains. This is a matter

of fact. Opinion: we are the portrait of a skyline

in progress. I need you to know that when it's summertime,

there will also be snow. I'm speechless

when I have booze-juice poured into a fancy cocktail

glass in front of me. That's a poor way of saying

nothing, and hello. Randomly, I wonder

about la señora selling mangos and strawberries

on a corner in Jackson Heights. I hope

she's okay. Suggestion: let us

return to our shores. Correction: Let us dream

of the magnificence of victory in our

thundersleep. Do not wake

yet. I am still here, holding on.

At the End of the World, All the Homies Pull Up to an Abandoned Gas Station in Alameda to Watch the Last Corpse Flower Bloom

What is every day if not a resistance
against an ending? I can't pretend like I know

the answer, but I know we were meant for this—a gentle
unfisting of petals despite the human industry

of failure. We have failed together. And we have endured
catastrophes. Both can be true at once. This isn't a testimony—

it's an invitation toward more. Because I don't want
what they've historically offered. Historically

nothing has been offered. I'm only spitting
what we already know to be true: that we are building

homes from the ashes of our ancestors; that we are
nurturing what we must; that we have always grown

from inside one another—like the time Rebeca
asked me to think of the happiest song I knew,

and when I couldn't think of one, she played me hers
while sitting on a porch beneath a disappearing West Oakland

sky. My people teach me about the smallest
liberations they've known, and it never includes a state-issued

response. Hernan says freedom feels like
drinking water at 3AM. It reminds me of all the tulips

dying right now, the uprooted
gardens. I'm calling upon

a radical blossoming, a generous
giving. I'll offer my labor, my limbs, if nothing

else. For now, let's remain
here: encircling ourselves, together and whole.

ACKNOWLEDGMENTS

To all the first-generation'ers out there. You're built different. For the times we've loved ourselves and the times we haven't.

Big props to the editors of the following publications for featuring versions of these poems in previous issues: *The Adroit Journal*; *Alien Magazine; Big Lucks; Bodega; Crab Fat Magazine; Dryland (*now *Sin Cesar); Empty Mirror; Flypaper Lit*; *Forum Literary Magazine; Gigantic Sequins; Honey Literary; Inner Forest Service; Juke Joint Mag; Kanstellation; Kissing Dynamite; The Normal School; [PANK]; Rust & Moth; Variety Pack; Your Impossible Voice.*

Shoutout to my pre-pandemic East Bay writers and homies. You saw the rawest versions of me through this project as I drafted, rambled, read, and revised many of these poems in our living rooms. I needed that nourishment in those moments. And you provided it. You know who you are. Fists up.

An especially big gracias to Michael Torres, Dorothy Chan, Sara Borjas, Gustavo Adolfo Barahona-Lopez, José Olivarez, Kim Sousa, Tess Taylor, and Matt Mitchell for your tenderness as humans, and your guidance—in different ways, times, and places—on this ever-evolving project.

To The Center for Cultural Power and Cristina Uribe for inviting me to contribute to the "Freedom to Vote" campaign. Thank you to Nix Guirre for your visual rendition of my poem "At the End of the World, All the Homies Pull Up to an Abandoned Gas Station in Alameda to Watch the Last Corpse Flower Bloom" (https://twitter.com/CultureStrike/status/1410643752469680130).

To my Oakland School for the Arts students and community, especially those who performed "16 Reasons Why a DACA Dreamer Will Be the First Person to Build a Do-It-Yourself Spaceship from Simple Materials" at the *Heart of Oakland* fundraiser inside the historic Fox Theater. It was an honor to share the stage with you all. This book is dedicated to you:

Noe Castrejon; Caleb Hassan-Amayo; Kwabena Stewart; Tristan Stewart; Richard Watson; and the future generations of pocho kids. Miss you all (https://www.youtube.com/watch?v=VMYpd8V-ln4).

To my wife Briana and our son Maceo, who is asleep while I'm writing this. These spaceships are for you. And there are more to be built.
With love.

ABOUT THE AUTHOR

Alan Chazaro is the author of *This Is Not a Frank Ocean Cover Album,* (Black Lawrence Press, 2019), *Piñata Theory* (Black Lawrence Press, 2020) and *Notes from the Eastern Span of the Bay Bridge* (Ghost City Press, 2021). He is a graduate of June Jordan's Poetry for the People program at UC Berkeley and a former Lawrence Ferlinghetti Poetry Fellow at the University of San Francisco. His work can be found in *GQ*, *National Pubic Radio*, *The Guardian*, *L.A. Times*, and more.